"Is This the Place?"

Letters from the Field

Leo Grillo

Dedication & Everlasting Love To Animals

DEDICATED
to the thousands of
abandoned animals who
will curl up on the cold ground to
sleep tonight. Scared and hungry, they
wonder what they did wrong.

Copyright 1995 by Leo Grillo

ALL RIGHTS RESERVED
PRINTED IN THE UNITED STATES OF AMERICA
FIRST EDITION

Table of Contents

Introduction: In memory of my Oscar	5
"He'd never seen another dog."	9
"She narrowly avoided a tragic ending."	13
"He listened in horror to the predators."	17
"He lay in the road for hours during our big earthquake."	21
"Our first wilderness dog after the earthquake."	25
"They were together in the forest for years."	29
"They hadn't had fresh water in months."	35
"Wake up! Wake up!"	39
"My Treasure, one man's trash."	41
"Longing to be touched."	45
"Foster mom, foster daughter."	49
"Heath was sent to us, I'm sure."	53

"He bravely led his brothers to safety."	57
"He never had a toy to call his own."	61
"Is this the place?"	65
"Severely wounded, she dragged herself to us for help."	73
"The one who stole my heart."	77
"Cold, hungry and wet."	81
"She thought I was going to hit her like the others."	85
"They said he was ugly and wouldn't touch him."	87
EPILOG	91
The History of D.E.L.T.A. Rescue	93
Preface to Guide	99
Pet Adoption Guide	101
About the Author	119
Tear-out Coupons	121

Introduction

In memory of my "Oscar"

Two days before this book was ready to go to the printer, a whole era in my life ended ... one of the first dogs I ever rescued, Oscar, died in my arms.

He was once a young, bouncy cocka-poo with a white shaggy coat and a face that would melt your heart. In his last few years, he didn't run or jump because of a bad left rear leg.

Last year, I think Oscar figured out that if he just lay down and let us wait on him, we would. So he did.

We had all kinds of vets examine him, X-ray him, Ultra Sound him, etc. None could explain why Oscar just decided to lie down a year ago! But I know he wanted to be a part of everything we did and that's why.

He lived in our hospital, in the middle of our busiest room. He was petted by everyone, constantly.

Eventually, Oscar couldn't see much, just shapes, shadows and light. But he could smell a dish of food a mile away! He'd let us sit him up and put the food in front of him ... then he'd feast.

Everyone gave Oscar treats ... roast beef was his favorite. Sliced turkey breast, chicken pieces, scrambled eggs, cottage cheese, cheeseburgers ... he loved them all!

I demand that all our animals be treated like people. *What else are they?* They have a different culture and a different language, but they think and feel and have the same emotions that we do. That makes them people in my book!

Especially Oscar.

He slept a lot in his last months. He'd awaken to food or for gentle petting.

He dreamed a lot, too. This moved me the most.

Oscar had a bad leg for about seven years. It prevented his running and jumping, which I know he loved.

But when Oscar dreamed, all four feet ran in his sleep and I know he was chasing leaves in the wind, re-living his youth. Some people might say that Oscar was "useless" because he couldn't fend for himself. But I know Oscar was enjoying his life with us and his dreams proved it.

In 1979 I found Oscar in the forest. He was injured by youths and was dumped, in pain, at a remote campsite.

It took weeks of feeding him for me to get near enough to slip a rope over his head. And he fought that rope with all his might ... but he was injured and I had to rescue him.

Oscar was among the very first dogs I found in the forest ... those thirty-five dogs who got me hooked for life.

Later, when Oscar was groomed for free by the "Bowser Boutique" on Melrose Ave. in Hollywood, he felt a lot better.

It was another week before Oscar stuck his head out from under my bed to let me pet him... he was so frightened of people.

But eventually, I won him over. He became my Delta's playmate. The two were inseparable until Delta died.

Oscar was the last of those original thirty-five dogs. As each one of my friends passed away, another arrow pierced my heart. And now that my beloved Oscar is gone too, I feel somehow much older than my forty-six years.

It's hard to watch your children die. But it's harder to walk away from them when they need your help. To help animals abandoned in the wilderness, I founded a non-profit organization called D.E.L.T.A. Rescue. The following chapters are copies of letters I've written over the years to D.E.L.T.A. Rescue supporters.

I rescued Oscar fifteen years ago ... I didn't write letters back then, so there isn't a chapter about him. That's why I wanted to tell you about him here. Oscar will always be with me as I walk amongst these forgotten animals.

> For the animals,
> Leo Grillo

Chapter 1

*"He'd never seen
another dog."*

September, 1994

Nobody wanted his love.

Instead they abandoned him ... left him to starve to death in the wilderness.

Though he looks intimidating with his wide, muscular head and penetrating gaze, Licks is a big puppy, giving hugs and kisses to anyone who'll have them.

When I first met him, he'd been eating from one of our feeding stations in the forest where he was abandoned.

Thanks to people like you, he didn't grow weaker from starvation everyday, give up hope and wait to die, like so many.

As I walked up to him, Licks ran into a bush.

He popped his head out to watch me as I got closer. He looked tough ... but his face softened and he smiled broadly as I put my hand out for him to sniff.

Then without warning, he lunged forward, blasting through the bush and he began kissing my hand.

Licks was so full of love I couldn't imagine someone throwing him away like this.

I scooped him up in my arms, and he hugged me back, as I carried him to our rescue van.

All during the drive to our sanctuary, Licks kissed my hand whenever I stuck it through his cage. And all during this trip, I asked myself why someone would abandon him.

As soon as we arrived at our shelter hospital, Licks was examined. He had a problem with his bladder, but simply neutering him would clear that up.

For the next few days, I visited Licks at our shelter. And right after he came out of surgery, I was there to tell him everything went fine.

"How's Licks?" I asked every time I talked to someone from the shelter. I couldn't stop thinking about him ... and why he loved everyone so much, after what was done to him.

Then the day came to take his picture for our loyal supporters.

I took Licks into a large exercise yard and tried to get a picture between kisses. I barely got a couple of shots off when suddenly, Licks ran off, disappearing behind a tree.

When I hiked over to the tree and looked around behind it, I saw something magical.

Very gently, Licks was touching his nose to the nose of another dog in the next yard, through the chain link fence. I could tell by the care he took with this dog, Licks hadn't seen another dog in a long time.

Licks had probably been kept tied in a yard alone, with nobody looking in on him or talking to him, not even another dog.

He was lonely, so very lonely. He just wanted someone to talk to ... someone to love him back.

That's why he was so thrilled when I held my hand out to him in the forest ... he had been alone for so long.

Licks couldn't get over this other dog being there! And when that dog went back to his own yard and a new one came out to exercise, Licks was just as fascinated with him.

So the dog that nobody wanted, who hoped for a friend for so long, and who was abandoned to die alone in the forest ... is safe now. And he is finally feeling loved himself.

Dear Leo,

I am sending a gift in the name of our three "throwaways."

Jake is a retired racing greyhound. Princess is a three year-old black cat we found when she was minutes old.

Chaser is a seven month-old kitten our three year-old daughter found at the babysitters. We are glad we took her home because a few days later her sibling was found dead in the street.

We wish you and your helpers well.

God bless you for what you do.

K.C.N.

Chapter 2

"She narrowly avoided a tragic ending"

August, 1994

Laura was a "bad" girl ... she got pregnant and had a litter of puppies that nobody wanted.

For this, she was sentenced to death!

Luke had a painful medical problem that would kill him. Its cure was a simple surgery, but that would cost money ... enough to buy two or three cases of beer.

Since he was going to die of it very soon, it would be better if he died out of sight ... alone, in the forest.

For their crimes against mankind, these two wonderful beings were abandoned in the wilderness, left to suffer pain, fear and hardship until they perished.

When I found them, huddled together under a tree in a forest picnic area, they were afraid of me.

As I approached them, slowly, Laura shivered and Luke protected her with his massive body, standing between us. He was in pain, slightly hunched over.

Sitting on the ground, I talked to them both for a while. Then Luke came over and kissed my hand. But Laura stayed against the tree and watched me.

Luke followed me to the van where I opened a large can of dog food, emptying the meat into two paper plates.

Seeing this, her hunger was too much for Laura! She ran over to me knowing she was going to have her first meal in days.

As I put the dishes on the ground and both dogs devoured the food, I ran my hand along Luke's back to reassure him. After he ate, Luke came over and gave me a big sloppy kiss and asked for more food.

Opening a second can, I asked Laura to come near too ... but she ran off again.

For the next hour I tried everything to rescue Laura.

I set out my cage trap and baited it ... Laura ate the food but shrewdly stepped around the trigger.

I sat under her tree for a long while, offering her bits of food. She ate from my fingers, but I couldn't get near enough to touch her.

I even put Luke in the van and kept the door open, so Laura could see him and know it was safe. That didn't work either.

Then I faced my dilemma: in order to get Luke medical treatment, I would have to rescue him now. But if I left Laura behind ... alone ... I might never see her alive again.

And if I left Luke behind, until I could catch Laura, which might not happen for days, Luke would die in agony from his medical condition.

Just when I was desperate, help came ... from Laura!

Somehow, she knew she might not see Luke again. This was too much for her to bear.

Nobody in this world had cared about her, she was thrown away like trash. And when she was at her lowest, Luke found her.

These dogs needed each other ... they just had to be together.

Boldly, Laura jumped into the van and ran up to Luke, kissing him as I closed the van door quickly.

"Thank you," I said to the powers that be. On the ride to our shelter, Laura sat next to Luke and they both smiled, knowing things were going to get better.

Thanks to people like you, Luke and Laura escaped disaster ... their support helped me be there for these precious animals.

At our 89-acre mountain top sanctuary, Luke had surgery immediately.

When he returned to Laura, he wagged his whole rear end with delight!

And she showered him with kisses!

Two lovers, losing everything in this world, only to find each other. This is the magic you too can be a part of!

Dear Leo and Staff,

I'm sorry my friend and I did not get to see you on the tour last month. I understand you had an emergency rescue to do.

The lady who took your place did a super job showing us around. She was so sweet.

I fell in love with all the dogs and cats, they are so wonderful.

I see where all the donations go!

Your animals are all so happy and your shelter is so clean.

Please keep up the beautiful job you do.

K.H.

Chapter 3

*"He listened in horror
to the predators."*

July, 1994

It was too dark for him to see, but Harpo felt the other kittens huddling with him for protection.

And then, one by one, they were pulled away.

Their tiny claws hung on to him as if he could save them. Their terror filled the air.

These attacks lasted all night. Harpo was too afraid to fall asleep. Then, with dawn, everything stopped.

All was quiet.

Harpo sniffed the air for his brothers and sisters, then he searched around for them under the bush.

This family of kittens that was cruelly abandoned in the forest. But they were all gone now ... except Harpo.

And this savage attack on his litter mates was the fourth such tragedy that I discovered in this particular wilderness campground lately.

You see, two weeks before Harpo was abandoned, three other litters of kittens went through the same frightening ordeal.

In the first incident, a mother and two kittens survived the predators. The rest of her children were lost.

In the second case, only a single kitten made it ... as if his whole family was ambushed.

When I rescued the survivor of the third massacre, my heart melted for him because he looked so sad and lonely.

I hoped he would be the last little guy to go through this.

Then, two weeks later, came Harpo ... walking slowly through some grass just after dawn, silently mouthing meows ... too weak to make a sound.

When I first picked him up, he purred and mouthed the meow word over and over.

I held him against my chest and he kneaded my shirt.

Harpo was so tiny. He miraculously survived the night attacks from predators, and I got him before he curled up and died of starvation.

I took Harpo home with me where I could give him constant care ... and where he could play with the four older kittens from the three litters abandoned there before his.

When I opened the first can of cat food for him, he went nuts! He squirmed and a hoarse meow came out of his mouth at the mere smell of the food.

I put a spoonful in his dish and he jumped in and gulped it right down.

As the days went by, his voice got better and better.

Now he meows with the others, and he can't wait for me to let him join them in running all over the laundry room.

Now I realize why nothing came out when he meowed, why I named him Harpo ... "the silent one."

He screamed in terror during the killings ... all night long, until he lost his voice. When I first held him, nothing came out because he was exhausted and all screamed out.

Then I thought ... what if you and I weren't here for him?

This poor little boy would have joined the others. He wouldn't have a chance to sit in our laps someday, all grown up and fluffy, kneading the air.

Being so small, nobody would have noticed if he was killed. And nobody would hear his silent cries.

But people like you were there with me ... we did save this little boy, and he will grow up and be safe and loved at our sanctuary.

Dear Leo,

My heart breaks for all those animals you write about. I would love to bring all of them home.

I hope you find a special home for Harpo and his friends, along with the rest of the animals.

Thanks for those home-made recipes for dogs and cats. They save me a fortune at the vets!

I have two dogs and one cat. I would like to have more recipes for my sixteen year old cat and one for my overweight three year old dog and my new puppy.

Keep up the good work. I'll pray for you.

R.S.

Chapter 4

"He lay in the road for hours during our big earthquake."

March, 1994

As each car shot past him on the road, the sound of the spinning wheels near his head made Roscoe tremble from fear.

He didn't want to be hurt again ... but he couldn't move out of the way ... he was paralyzed.

And the ground rumbled and quaked over and over, bouncing Roscoe up and down, banging his head against the curb.

Yet he fought on, *determined* to live through it all, somehow.

Finally, someone saw him and called the pound.

Then, on day two of the quake, when the telephones opened up for a few short minutes, I managed to talk to the supervisor of the city pound and told him D.E.L.T.A. Rescue would send medical supplies and veterinarians to his facility, immediately.

Just moments after my call, Roscoe arrived there. Normally, he would have been killed immediately. Instead, he was seen by one of the vets that we hired to help these earthquake animals.

Roscoe's neck was broken.

There was little hope of his ever walking again. It was even impossible for him to raise his head to drink.

This magnificent, healthy four-year-old black lab was doomed.

After all he'd been through, nothing could be done.

I thought about ordering Roscoe the special Canine Cart. We've used it on a number of crippled dogs with wonderful success.

I could order Roscoe a special version of the cart, one that would support him upright with four wheels.

We'd push him around the shelter to visit the other dogs and we'd spoil him ... giving him the best life we could.

But still, it was sad. He was so young and he'd been through so much already ... left for dead by the side of the road ... in the middle of a killer quake.

Hoping for a miracle, I had Roscoe's X-rays sent over to a young orthopedic specialist I'd heard of. But he only confirmed the gloomy diagnosis.

But, he added, that *without* surgery Roscoe was *guaranteed* a life of paralysis.

With it, there was at least a tiny chance he would eventually get *some* movement back ... maybe enough to sit up when he ate.

So all I could do was make the arrangements ... long distance ... because the freeways had collapsed between our shelter and Los Angeles.

I wasn't prepared for what happened next.

Roscoe was moved to the new hospital and had his operation, immediately. Then the surgeon called me.

I can still hear his words in my head.

He said that Roscoe woke up from the surgery, looked around, and then stood up on all fours.

We got our miracle!

After all his suffering ... he made it. Roscoe would walk again!

As soon as I could, I drove to the hospital ... and I met this precious dog who had been only a dream until now.

When I first saw him I was overwhelmed.

Roscoe wagged his tail and lifted his head, as much as he could, and smiled at me ... as if we were old friends!

I hugged him and promised him the best life possible at our 89-acre Supershelter.

And that's what he's getting now. Going for long walks and pulling us along side ... running up to the hospital refrigerator for treats ... he's having a ball!

Thanks to people like you, we saved Roscoe and over 40 other sick and injured dogs and cats from the 6.7 Northridge Earthquake.

But the extra expense is draining us.

More than ever, I need your support as we try to make ends meet in caring for all 750 of our animals. Plus 41 more!

Dear Leo,

I am enclosing a donation. We are retired and are on a limited income but will help when we can.

We really admire your work and try to emulate you in our neighborhood by being there for the lost and homeless.

We once found a dog with a tag from Phoenix, Arizona, and called to find the owner here.

We have two dogs from Escondido, Mexico. The puppy we have had his mother with him. She had mange. We took them both, I couldn't bring myself to leave one behind.

We also have a very old cat that we adopted. He sat in our back yard and decided we belonged to him. We do our best when we can and never send any animal to the pound.

We love your letters. They are so moving. God bless you and your staff for caring so much.

B.B.

Chapter 5

***"Our first wilderness dog
after the earthquake."***

May, 1994

Terry is magnificent, proud and playful. But he wasn't always like that ....

Just a few days before he was a cowering, frightened dog who slinked across our hospital floor, his tail between his legs.

You see, Terry was another victim of the big earthquake. Access roads to the forest were cut off so nobody could drive to picnic areas or camp grounds to abandon their pets.

But they didn't have to.

With all the confusion and animals loose from fallen block wall fences, anyone could drive to the San Fernando Valley and dump their pets.

There, they wandered the streets aimlessly ... joining the other strays, trying to find their way home again ... only to be hit by cars.

Maybe Terry's family tried to dump him the same way. Maybe he kept finding his way home again.

Whatever he went through during the earthquakes,

when the roads to the forest finally re-opened, Terry was driven to a campground and booted out of the car.

I know he hadn't eaten in weeks when I found him. He was all bone under his long coat, and he was very tired.

Terry was hiding under a bush when I rescued him and took him to our shelter.

He huddled in a corner of the van during the hour's drive. He was so afraid to make a wrong move that he didn't move at all.

"What horror has this poor dog been through?" I wondered.

At our hospital, when anyone came near, he turned away and buried his head in a corner of his cage and shivered.

But we showered him with love and special attention, and in a few days, he was more trusting. Eventually he went for short walks on a lead.

Next, we put him out into a covered yard. It wasn't long before he figured out he was safe, and he was loved.

Terry blossomed in this newfound love ... playing ball every day with his caretaker, and splashing in his pool.

When I took him into one of our large exercise yards to play with him, I couldn't get over how happy he was. He danced all the way to the yard and when I let him run loose, he jumped all over me ... kissing and hugging me as if he was trying to thank me for helping him.

When I held Terry and patted his head and looked into his smiling eyes, I couldn't help but see what could have happened to him ... his thin, lifeless body lying there, under a bush, while the world went on without his loving presence.

I've seen enough to know how it works.

If you really love an animal, he will live for you, as long as you love him. Terry knows how loved he is now.

Dear Leo,

I want to thank you for all you did during the earthquakes for our poor animals.

Sending veterinarians and loads of medicine to the two pounds really helped. As you know, at your request, no animals were put to sleep for at least the first month following the quake, as long as you were needed there.

This allowed plenty of time for owners to find their pets and for people to adopt the poor animals that were the forgotten victims of homeless families.

I read where Mayor Riordan and the city council gave D.E.L.T.A. Rescue a citation of appreciation for all you did for the animals.

Congratulations and God bless you.

H.K.

Chapter 6

"They were together in the forest for years."

September, 1993

At first, they ate only after I drove off.

But over the next few weeks, they got used to me and even looked forward to my visits with them in the forest.

Soon they began wagging their tails when they saw me coming with their food!

I'd been doing this for weeks.

Girlie, a shepherd mix, was terribly shy and she would slink behind Old Yellow with her tail low. She followed him everywhere.

Old Yellow, a lab, always ate first while Girlie watched. If she felt it was safe, she'd take her turn.

But if Old Yellow got frightened and ran off without finishing his meal, Girlie would run off too ... going without any food just to be with him.

This one morning, I noticed Old Yellow was injured, walking very slowly ... on his tiptoes ... and in a lot of pain.

I had to get him to the hospital. That meant I had to rescue him quickly, and the only safe way was with our large cage-trap.

Because Girlie would be left behind in the forest, alone, if I rescued Old Yellow, I hadn't used the trap before this. But now there was no choice. If he didn't get help quickly, Old Yellow could end up paralyzed.

I set the trap near the two dogs and baited it with fresh hamburger meat. Old Yellow tiptoed right in and the door slammed shut.

But as it closed, the rattling noise it made frightened poor Girlie and she ran off into the brush.

Meanwhile I got Old Yellow to the hospital. X-rays showed his tail had been shot off, and he had over 100 shotgun pellets still in his body, from an old injury.

Imagine the pain he'd been through, lying under a bush, bleeding ... Girlie helplessly comforting him. No wonder she never left his side.

Feeling her desperation now, I returned to rescue her too. But she was nowhere in sight.

I couldn't sleep that night worrying about her ... all alone in the wilderness, frightened.

So before dawn I went back to the forest with a fresh supply of hamburger meat and our trap ... hoping to find her.

I didn't have to wait long. As I was unloading my equipment, Girlie quietly came right up behind me, her tail wagging.

I reached out to her. She came close, but stayed out of range. So I set the trap.

Trusting me ... she walked right in!

Back at our sanctuary I reunited these two friends. Tails wagged, kisses flew ... and there was a lot of dancing!

Animals fall in love, just like people. I've seen it over and over.

Girlie loved Old Yellow, and when she saw him, she exploded in joy ... kissing him and running in circles around him, then kissing him some more!

Old Yellow was hurting. He smiled at her and wagged his tail too ... but moving too much hurt his back.

Our veterinarian put him on medicine for pain, caused by arthritis from all the gunshot wounds. Within weeks, he was walking briskly again.

And the two are inseparable.

I took Old Yellow and Girlie out last night, into one of our huge exercise yards.

He followed me everywhere, thanking me for saving his life .

Girlie was always just behind him, and for one little moment ... there was a bit of magic.

Maybe she was intoxicated by the evening light, or maybe she was just so full of joy from being back with Old Yellow.

But Girlie came up to me, quickly, while I was bending over to rub Old Yellow's neck ... and she licked my hand.

She brought tears to my eyes.

This was the greatest reward she could have ever

given me ... her love.

All the early mornings and sleepless nights, the aches and pains of working in the wilderness ... the worrying.

It all goes away when you can change fate and save animals like Old Yellow and Girlie ... and have their unconditional love.

Because people like you support this mission by sending a gift each month, I can feed dogs like Old Yellow and Girlie in the wilderness where they're dumped. I can gain their trust, no matter how long it takes, and bring them to our sanctuary.

Old Yellow and Girlie are lucky. Thanks to people who care, they had plenty to eat while they were out there.

It wasn't like that when I first started ... back in 1979. I still remember that morning as if it were yesterday ....

Sadly, I found 35 dogs in the forest that morning.

They were so hungry they knocked over garbage cans full of picnic trash ... trying to find a morsel of food. They even ate paper sandwich wrappers.

I was so shaken by this, I drove to the city and bought four large fifty pound bags of dog food.

Once back in the forest, I spread them over the ground.

Then I whistled for the dogs — they ran toward my car ... all 35 of them! What a sight! I can still see their faces ... all my old friends.

They dove into the food piles up to their elbows and started munching loudly. And while they ate, they smiled at me ... thanking me for helping them.

Moved to tears, I never left their side.

We were together in the cold, winter rains — when they were sick with pneumonia and I put medicine in their food to help them get through it.

I remember feeling so helpless that I couldn't do more for them.

My best friends were homeless, living on the cold ground ... trying to sleep through the pounding storms in puddles of water — rain beating constantly on their heads.

It took a full year to get them all out of the forest, but I did ... before the next winter's rains.

I found loving homes for some, but many I kept myself. I was too much in love with them to say "goodbye."

Most have gone now ... just telling you about them, the tears well up in my eyes. I miss them terribly.

I didn't start out to build the only dog and cat wilderness rescue organization in the country ... it just happened, because of these 35 beautiful dogs.

And as each one passed away over the years, my sadness became a renewed commitment to dedicate my life to saving their friends, whatever it takes.

Dear Leo,

Enclosed is a picture of Benji. He will be twelve in May

He is a sweet, lovable dog and more precious to us each day.

We can't thank you enough for rescuing him and letting us adopt him almost twelve years ago. Of course, we miss his brother, Lucky, whom we lost five years ago to cancer.

We thank God we had the chance to share our lives with them both.

J .& P .H.

Chapter 7

"They hadn't had fresh water in months."

April, 1990

National Geographic wanted to feature my rescue work in their TV-special about cats.

I hoped this episode would inspire others to rescue abandoned cats as well, so I agreed to do it.

Weeks later, I took the film crew to an ocean breakwater. Two cats were abandoned there, without food or water.

When I first found him, a tabby cat I named "Jet" ran from cave to cave beneath my feet ... following me as I jumped from boulder to boulder along the huge ocean jetty.

"Marina," his black female friend, stayed back and watched ... until I cut a hole in the jug I was carrying.

Fresh water dripped down its side and onto some sharp coral-like rocks below.

Both cats raced down to the jagged coral and licked it furiously ... it was only a few drops, but they couldn't remember when they had fresh water last.

When I put the container down on the jetty, they climbed back up the boulders, and stuck both of their heads into the jug opening.

It was the first drink they had since they were abandoned, months before. They drank ... and drank.

For weeks, I returned to care for Jet and Marina. Whenever I got out onto the jetty, the cats would run out to the farthest point and wait for their water.

When the weather got bad and the seas got rough, the pounding surf and spray soaked Jet and Marina ... and they caught colds.

They had no peace from the thundering waves, and no dry, warm bed to sleep in.

I had to trap them to take them to the safety of our sanctuary.

I tried all kinds of food as bait to get Jet and Marina to go into the cage traps ... but they were too smart.

Meanwhile, the weather got worse.

When National Geographic sent their TV crew to meet me in the field, I told them about Jet and Marina.

Willing to brave the treacherous jetty, not to mention high winds and surf, National Geographic set up their cameras.

But after trying for hours to rescue these two cats, nothing was happening. They were too afraid.

Then I had a hunch. Instead of food, I put water inside the traps for bait. It worked on Jet.

The smell of the fresh water was too much for this poor animal to resist.

He was afraid to be caught, but he threw caution to the wind. With cameras rolling, Jet inched his way into the trap ... and lapped up the water.

When he stepped on the trigger plate, the cage door came down. He flinched ... but he never stopped drinking.

When he finally finished and started cleaning himself, I carried him to our rescue van.

National Geographic filmed Jet's entire rescue, and later, aired it nationally. With the weather so bad and the jetty so dangerous, I asked them to leave.

But Marina was still out there, and I couldn't just leave her alone. Like Girlie with Old Yellow ... Marina desperately needed Jet.

When I went back out to get her, she was more frightened than ever, and she stayed away from me, hiding in the rocks.

For hours I sat there in the cold mist, pleading with her to let me take her to Jet.

Then, when we were both exhausted, an amazing thing happened.

I told her she could have all the water she wanted, for the rest of her life, if she only came home with me now.

She seemed to understand.

And when I told her Jet was waiting in the van, and they would live happily together at our huge sanctuary, Marina blinked to me.

Then she spoke to me with a soft meow ... and walked right into the trap.

That moment, when the trap door shut, I had to hold down the lump in my throat. What a happy moment ... I had both cats at once! They wouldn't be separated.

At our sanctuary, Marina and Jet live together, in love, rubbing their heads together and drinking lots of cool, fresh water.

Their story has a happy ending because some people care.

And like other D.E.L.T.A. Rescue supporters, you have the power to stop a terrible tragedy.

You can be the difference between life and death for other abandoned cats, like Marina and Jet.

Chapter 8

"Wake up!
Wake up!"

January, 1994

It happened sometime before 6:20 on Saturday morning ... most likely in the bone-chilling dark of night ... someone abandoned a litter of six-week-old puppies in the woods.

When I found these shivering puppies they were huddled together in a small laundry basket. During that miserable night, one of the little boys got too cold, and he died of exposure.

My heart just ached as I first saw these frightened little faces staring up at me, sadly ... hungry and cold, wondering whether or not I would be the one to help them.

Whoever did this crossed the line with me!

Yes, I've been rescuing abandoned animals for 15 years. And I've never understood why it happens to these loving creatures.

And yes, I've rescued many litters of helpless puppies before.

But this bunch really got to me.

When I saw them not only stare at their dead

brother with sad eyes, but go over to him and lick his face, begging him to wake up ... it r i p p e d m y h e a r t o u t and made me very angry at the same time.

"They won't get away with this" I promised the puppies. "I will see that they're prosecuted ... for abandoning you and killing your little brother."

I am still very angry! This cruelty must stop and you and I must do something to stop it! You must join me in getting angry at the people committing cowardly crimes like this.

Immediately, I called the local newspapers and offered them the story about a $500 reward for information leading to the arrest and conviction of the person who committed this crime against these innocent puppies.

For fifteen years I've been rescuing these starving animals, but the abandonment continues. I have to do more.

So I made up $500 Reward posters and we're now handing them out in the area where the pups were dumped ... hoping to find the person responsible.

When we do locate the criminal, I'll turn the case over to the county for prosecution. Fines could be over $36,000 plus jail time for nine counts each of cruelty to animals and abandonment.

Once the public sees that we're helping enforce the existing abandonment laws, they'll know that abandonment is not only immoral, but is also punishable as well.

Chapter 9

"My Treasure, one man's trash!"

August, 1993

While on a dog rescue mission a few weeks ago, a ranger friend of mine flagged me down. He said someone had thrown some kittens away ... in a trash dumpster.

One of the park workers was throwing the trash away and he saw something squirming under some papers. He peeled away the garbage and found four two-hour old kittens.

They were all crying weakly ... and were hypothermic.

When I got there, I filled up an empty soda bottle with hot water and draped the four limp little bodies over it. Then I raced to our shelter where I could put them in an incubator.

At our shelter hospital all four kittens began crying for their mother. They were coming out of shock and were hungry.

One at a time, we nursed them from a bottle and placed them in a warm towel inside the incubator. This went on every few hours for several days.

Sadly, one by one, three of the little kittens died. This last one was a little bigger and he ate with gusto, but he too was fading. When I saw he wasn't going to make it, I took him home where I could personally give him intensive, round the clock care.

Looking at his tiny body curled up in the palm of my hand, I imagined him all grown up ... he'd be a huge Maine Coon cat. He'd chase after me when I left the room, and he'd purr loudly when I held him close.

He'd sit on the window sill and watch the squirrels and birds. And he'd never be homeless or unwanted again.

I desperately wanted him to live, to grow, to know happiness. So I whispered into his ear, over and over again, that if he lived, he'd be my own special cat ... my "Treasure."

At every meal, I held him up to my face and talked to him, and kissed him. Then I gave him his warm bottle.

After his bottle I held him some more, whispering to him, telling him to stay with me. Days passed ... he was still weak. But he'd crawl to me ... stumbling over his towel ... when he heard me opening his incubator lid to feed him.

I'd see little improvements everyday. He'd crawl a little faster ... he'd eat a little more.

One day, the very corners of his eyelids began to open. Finally he could see his "grandpa!" He stared at me while he purred and sucked down his milk, pulling his bottle closer with tiny little hands.

After he ate, I whispered "Hello, little guy" into his ear and let him look into my eyes for the first time. I kissed him and he rubbed his face all over my nose, purring constantly, as if to say "Thank you."

Then one morning it was the moment of truth.

I held my breath as I put a spoonful of solid cat food out for him. I felt tears of relief when he dived into the food and took his first bites. He'd made it. My little Treasure would live!

Treasure plays in our laundry room all day now. He loves to toss our socks in the air! At night he sleeps with his stuffed football-pillow in the laundry basket.

Thanks to people like you, I was able to be there for Treasure. And thanks to people like you, he'll live a long and happy life.

Treasure epilog ...

My Treasure grew up big and strong. He lives with my wife, myself and our daughter.

Though we have over two dozen cats and eight dogs at home, Treasure knows he's very special.

He's the only one to sleep in our bedroom all day.

In the morning, his favorite thing to do is climb the window above our bed, open the shutters, and stare out at the birds, bunnies and squirrels.

When we go to bed at night, Treasure rubs his head all over us and we rub his face in return ... just like we did when he was an infant with his eyes closed.

I can't believe we share the planet with people who abandon animals. They have no idea how special these lives are, how pure and innocent.

Then I feel sorry for them.

They will never know the peace and love we share with Treasure.

Chapter 10

"Longing to be touched."

December, 1992

I'd pull the van near one of my forest feeding stations and begin opening cans of dog food.

Out of the brush dogs would come running. Five or six would gather around me and as quickly as I put the food on the ground, a couple of them would sneak in and inhale it.

My job was pitching the food so that each dog got his share.

Then I'd look up and in the distance would be this old dog, stiffly walking along the trail ... hurrying to come to dinner.

I named him Bruno.

When Bruno finally got to me, I'd have to pitch some food out behind me so the other dogs would run over there. Then I'd toss Bruno his share, which he ate slowly ... gentlemanly.

Whenever I showed up the dogs would expect my canned food feast and would gather around the van. One or two at a time I'd be able to touch them, pick them up, and put them in the van for the trip to our shelter.

But Bruno always stayed just out of reach.

This went on for months.

I rescued a lot of dogs in this one area, a campsite next to the forest. But never Bruno.

Watching him walk toward me, gray around the muzzle, I wondered who abandoned him and why.

Every time I fed him I couldn't help but feel his longing to be touched.

He'd watch me hug the other dogs and he'd just look up, sadly. My heart always ached for him.

Months passed and Bruno ate regularly, and he had plenty of dry food to nibble on between my visits ... but I could never get close enough to help him.

I desperately wanted to rescue Bruno, especially after I took his friend Buster, a lab cross he hung around with, to our shelter.

Now Bruno was alone, and the weather turned cold. I couldn't sleep knowing he was out there while I was in a warm bed.

My special cage trap was the only chance we both had. But Bruno was smart and I didn't know if he'd walk into it.

Early one morning I set the trap. When I opened the familiar can of food, Bruno came out of a bush and walked up to me. He watched as I loaded the trap with his favorite treat. Then I casually walked away while he went up to it and began eating.

Five times he entered the trap and was not caught. I held my breath each time because if he tripped the door before he was in all the way, it would close ... but he could escape backwards. If this happened, I knew he would never go in again.

Finally, my prayers were answered. He went all the way in and tripped the door. I had him!

Running up to the trap, I hugged the cage with Bruno in it. He calmed right down.

On the ride to our shelter we had a long "talk."

My feelings were that Bruno was a "junk yard" guard dog. He'd never known the love and tenderness of a real family ... or a gentle touch.

Bruno spent his whole life as a "watch dog" and when he was too old and too stiff to work anymore, he was taken "for a ride."

Now at our shelter, for the first time in his life, he's loved and cared for. And he doesn't have to "earn" his keep.

Bruno is still afraid of people, but every day he trusts a little more. He took treats from my fingers the other day, and when he first saw me in the distance, I caught him ... he wagged his tail twice!

But when I turned in his direction he tucked it under again. I know he likes me and I'll work for the day when I can finally hug him.

Thanks to people like you, I could spend many months rescuing Bruno. With your support I can continue this work.

Bruno Epilog ...

Today Bruno has a huge yard, a dog house of his own and a "club house" to share with his female companion.

These two follow each other everywhere ... they eat, sleep and play together.

Bruno's yard is closest to the edge of our property, next to virgin mountain-top wilderness. So he gets to see lots of rabbits, coyotes, deer and the occasional mountain lion. Bruno loves these visits!

And I swear ... he's younger today than when I rescued him.

Chapter 11

***"Foster mom,
foster daughter."***

June, 1992

"Chelsea," a yellow lab mix who was a new mom and still full of milk, was taken away from her home and left in a wilderness picnic area, on a Monday.

She ran around looking everywhere for her four-week-old babies.

Panic-ridden, she stopped only to eat the food at one of our D.E.L.T.A. Rescue feeding stations in the forest.

She was full of milk and her breasts began to hurt by Monday night.

Chelsea stayed out in the woods that night, curled up in a ball under a picnic table. Every wild sound reminded her of her missing pups.

As much as I wish I could, I can't rescue dogs like Chelsea on their first day, in case their puppies were dumped too ... hidden under a bush or tree somewhere.

Tuesday. No puppies were seen anywhere. Chelsea ate and stopped her frantic search of all the brush. Maybe the pups weren't dumped.

Wednesday. Still no puppies. Chelsea began to stay in one spot ... near the food we provided for her. Thin but loving, she wagged her tail as she ate from the pile of kibble.

Thursday. Chelsea still had plenty of milk, but no puppies. After three days of waiting for a dog to lead me to her litter, I can be sure there isn't one. What happened to those innocent little creatures?

From her condition I could guess that Chelsea's pups were now about four weeks old. At this age the pups are still infants, barely able to walk. They need their mother for at least another four weeks.

Chelsea was lonely, wondering how this could have happened to her.

She carried her babies for nine weeks, she delivered them one night by herself, fed them and cleaned them from head to tail, around the clock for a month.

She watched them grow, open their eyes, stumble around and begin to get their "legs."

They loved her, running to her when their eyes met.

She watched them begin to play with each other, tugging at passing tails, rolling around and stopping only to nurse or nap.

She was content. They were a happy family.

Then came Monday ....

Chelsea's pups were taken from her and she was loaded into the family car for one last ride.

On Friday, in another tragic situation, "Cassie" was abandoned in the same area.

She is a seven-week-old puppy, frightened to be

away from her litter mates ... and her mom.

Wandering aimlessly, Cassie caught sight of Chelsea and was following her when I showed up that morning.

I picked up the little puppy and held her in my arms. When I kissed Cassie's face, Chelsea came over and wagged her tail, waiting for me to hug her too.

Petting Chelsea, I got an idea.

I put the hungry puppy up to Chelsea's face. They kissed.

So I put little Cassie under Chelsea and lifted her to a breast ... she immediately wolfed down her breakfast.

Chelsea knew the ritual. After the baby ate, she cleaned her and nuzzled her for a while. They were bonding as only two dogs who really needed each other could.

Chelsea was a mom who lost her kids, and Cassie was an orphan. Now they were a family.

I watched as Chelsea began schooling her little one on how to behave. It's amazing. She's a smart dog and had lots to teach her pups. Now, thanks to people like you, she has a chance ... she has Cassie.

Without our help, Chelsea and Cassie would have become just tragic statistics. But we were there, and we've helped make another happy ending.

You can work miracles and be the answer to another animal's prayer for help. Team up with me, let's stop the suffering and help these animals.

Dear Leo,

I felt so sorry for Chelsea being taken away from her babies.

I wonder what ever happened to her puppies ... probably sold for beer money or given away at a supermarket.

But to know she helped poor Cassie makes me feel like I really made the difference this month.

Keep up the rescuing.

I'm on social security, but here's a little extra for these two dogs anyway. Please buy them some special treats from me.

W.P.

Chapter 12

*"Heath was sent
to us, I'm sure."*

June, 1993

One morning I got a call from a park ranger. Some campers had carried an injured five month old puppy to his truck while he was on patrol.

As the sun went down the night before, a strange car came racing into the wilderness picnic area where these people were camping.

Making dust tracks everywhere, the speeding car's window came rolling down and a body was thrown out into the brush.

With a scream, and loud piercing cries, Heath smashed into the ground and rolled endlessly, coming to a stop against a tree trunk near one of our forest feeding stations.

As the car sped off, the witnesses went over to this hurt puppy and put a blanket under him. Then they carried him to their campfire and took him to my ranger friend the next morning.

An hour later, Heath was at our Supershelter hospital.

He had four fractured ribs and a badly lacerated left arm.

Heath had surgery and slept all of his first day with us.

I drove to the hospital at two the next morning, to check on him and I ended up spending the rest of the night there.

He was very depressed and had "the look" in his eyes. Heath had Parvo too.

He was thrown out of a moving car ... deathly ill. His painful injuries disguised his disease.

With all that had happened to him, I was worried he wouldn't live.

Heath suffered a lot.

For days, every time he vomited from Parvo, his fractured ribs made him scream out in pain.

Not eating, his small body lay there, wasting away. It felt hopeless.

I kept picturing what Heath could have been ... a happy German Shepherd, running the hills, chasing balls ... smiling all the time ... loved by someone all his own.

Instead, he was dying in this hospital cage, knowing only abuse and suffering.

So I made Heath a promise as he looked up at me with those sad brown eyes ... one that I knew he understood.

If somehow he could fight a while longer, and live, I would get him the best new home any dog could ask for. His own home, where he'd be the joy of someone's life ... someone who would appreciate his enormous depth and sensitivity.

Every day Heath fought to hang on.

Then, little by little, I saw his eyes brighten.

One week after his trauma, he wagged his tail at me, rolling over on his side in his cage.

I knew he'd turned the corner.

Days later he was bright and alert and he began eating up a storm!

He made it! And I kept my promise ....

Twelve years before, I rescued a wonderful German Shepherd named "Heather" from the mountains where she was shot ... in the *left front leg*.

One of my best friends, a famous Hollywood acting coach, fell in love with her right away and adopted her. And he nursed her through many surgeries.

Heather was the love of his life, and he was devastated by her loss last September.

I know how depressed he was.

Talking about another dog was out of the question. So I mailed him some polaroids of Heath.

Heather and Heath looked identical. He cried when he saw the pictures.

It was as if Heather had sent Heath to him, to take her place. And in case we didn't realize who he was, Heath's *left front leg* was badly hurt, too. It was sort of a signal.

My friend planned for days to adopt Heath. Every timed he talked to me he sounded younger than his seventy years. He came alive again.

When he met Heath, the two fell in love immediately. They've been inseparable ever since.

My friend calls me now and then to update me ... and to tell me how smart Heath is. It was as if Heath knew the house and all the routines. As if he'd been there before!

Thanks to people like you, I was able to be there for Heath, and even for my friend in his grief. They are both healed now, and somehow, a part of us is healed too.

It all works when we realize we are all connected ... to each other, to the planet ... and to the animals.

By helping the animals, we help ourselves, too.

D.E.L.T.A. Rescue is for us as well as the animals. The more you help this mission, the more you help yourself. Please be very generous.

Chapter 13

"He bravely led his brothers to safety."

October, 1994

Their mother didn't come home all day, and they were very hungry.

But when she didn't return at night either, they starved ... in the cold ... just twenty feet from the ocean.

By morning, three of the tiny kittens died of exposure and starvation. Columbus, born with a tough survival instinct, knew he had to do something to save the rest....

I got to the railroad tracks near the beach about noon.

There, crawling slowly, but with fierce determination, was little Columbus. He was a three-week-old orange kitten making his way through the grass as if it were a forest.

Stumbling along behind him were his two brothers, a gray long-haired kitten and a frail white one. When I saw how skinny they were, I knew their mother was young and didn't have enough milk for them all.

As I picked up each kitten to put him in a box, he

meowed to me telling me his tragic story. I held each one under my chin for a moment, trying to comfort him.

When I poured a jar of baby food into a paper dish, they waded into it and began sucking ... it felt so good to eat something.

Columbus' mother must have been abandoned at this site when she was pregnant. Her kittens were born in the wild, and were covered with giant fleas.

But she was gone now ... either tragically, or else she was picked up by a camper who didn't know she had kittens out there. After all, she had to be lovable, her children are.

Columbus and his brothers slept during the two hour ride home. I kept the heater on in the car to be sure they warmed up from the cold, damp ocean air.

When I got them home, the first thing we did was spray them with flea killer and then give them a warm bath.

After we dried them, the kittens were put in a heated box with a fluffy new towel.

Exhausted from their ordeal, they curled up together and went to sleep.

Like a proud father, I watched them as they slept, warm and safe now, and with full tummies. And I admired their courage.

Brave little Columbus, their hero, who led them through the heavy grass to safety ... such a huge life in such a teeny package.

And the gray one who looks at you with wide-open innocent eyes, hoping for a chance to be loved.

Then the sad one, the white one who was the skinniest of the three ... and always the last one in line. I kept imagining him all grown up ... magnificent and heavy.

All three kittens were so small they all fit in the palm of my hand ... yet they moved me so much I couldn't bear the thought of losing one.

And in the shape they were in, that was something that could happen.

But with intensive, round-the-clock nursing, they all pulled through. Thanks to the support of people like yourself, these orphaned little boys who were within hours of death, will live.

Without us, what chance did these kittens have?

I only wish I could have rescued their mother too. Then maybe I could have saved their beautiful little sisters.

But, even these three babes would have died, unnoticed by anyone in their well hidden den ... except for Columbus, and us.

Columbus epilog,

As I write this today, Columbus, Caesar (the white one) and Napoleon are all running around the house being curious, playful kittens.

They all made it and they're all so lovable.

Columbus is still the brave one, exploring everything first.

Caesar is the big eater in the family. He's also the one who jumps on your shoulder to lick your neck and suck on your hair!

Nappy is the musher ... he curls up and purrs next to your face and he's in heaven when you rub his tummy.

They have a younger litter to play with, from another beach. I've kept all six of these kittens at home because they all needed my personal intensive care.

It helps when the same person does it round the clock, so any subtle changes can be observed.

I don't sleep much during kitten season!

For my forty-sixth birthday next week, Stacy asked what I wanted. I wrote it down and left the room:

"Columbus, Caesar, Napoleon, Tammy, Roscoe and Bruiser."

I know I can't have them all ... that's what our shelter is for. But maybe just three! We'll see next week.

Chapter 14

*"He never had a toy
to call his own."*

December, 1994

Sherwood was the puppy nobody wanted, so they gave him nothing ... not a kind word, not a loving touch ... nothing.

When all the other puppies were taken, and nobody bought Sherwood, he was driven out to the wilderness and abandoned. And he was only five months old!

For over a week, Sherwood hid in the brush, running deeper into it if anyone came near ... he was deathly afraid of people.

But thanks to our supporters, at least little Sherwood didn't starve.

One of our feeding stations was nearby, and Sherwood found it.

Now he had food ... but nothing more.

Then one morning a week later, something strange happened.

Nearby campers said Sherwood had been elusive, slipping in and out of the brush but never coming near anyone, until about an hour before I arrived that magical day.

They tell me that Sherwood came out of the brush, and sat on the dirt road as if he was waiting for someone.

If anyone approached him, he'd run off, only to return to the same spot a few minutes later.

And then I arrived.

When I pulled our rescue van up to my usual spot in the road, I saw Sherwood for the first time.

Getting out of the van, I knelt down and called to him. He came right over to me and let me pet him. Then I picked him up and put him on the front seat next to me.

Campers said they couldn't believe it ... they jokingly said "this dog must be waiting for Leo to come."

Then I did!

There's something very special about Sherwood. He has a look of sadness and distrust ... a depth born of suffering. And yet he has strength, pride and courage.

I never knew what my Delta looked like as a puppy. He was the first dog I rescued in the wilderness in 1979, and he was two-years-old and full grown.

I often wondered what he was like as a puppy. Now I know. Sherwood looks exactly like baby Delta, returned to me after all these years of missing him.

Now Sherwood has food, shelter and love. And yet, there must be something more.

And we have 750 other very special cats and dogs just like Sherwood. They were all abandoned and none of them had a toy to call their own, until we rescued them. But I want them to have something more.

So I came up with an idea ....

Let's give Christmas stockings full of treats and toys to each one of our cats and dogs this Christmas!

Their own stocking full ... now that's something more!

Help me show them how much we love each and every one of them. After you send your best gift to help rescue, feed and care for our animals, do something extra ... sponsor a Christmas stocking for a dog or cat!

Baby Sherwood will get the first stocking on Christmas morning, then all the others will get theirs!

On Christmas morning, your stockings and your love will be given to some very grateful animals.

Dear Leo,

I really enjoyed filling out those gift tags knowing you put them on my Christmas stockings that I sponsored for the cats and dogs.

And your answering my letter and telling me about "Schotzie" was great.

I feel so good knowing that my stockings were given to her. What a remarkable dog, to have cancer and to keep eating and walking around. Telling me about her enjoying several treats at a time from her stockings made my day.

And good for you -- to take extra stockings and hang them just for her.

I know you're right -- if we want them to live, and shower them with love and joy, they will. Schotzie is proof positive!

I hope we do this every year, I'm already planning on sponsoring more than the five stockings I did next Christmas.

G.D.

Chapter 15

"Is this the place?"

January, 1992

When I first saw her, I was driving up a back country road that runs through the forest.

It's a fast, well traveled old highway. Cars kill lots of wildlife on this road.

From my left I could see her coming out of the mountains, and in my rear view mirror I could see her crossing that deadly road.

She made it across and headed for some bushes where she rested her weary body.

When I pulled over and began walking towards her, Bebe got scared and ran off, up a hill.

I drove home to get our fully-equipped rescue van and some supplies, then returned to hunt for Bebe.

Meanwhile, she struggled on, searching for that place in her heart where all would be well.

I drove to higher ground, up a windy mountain road. Four miles later, Bebe came out of the forest, walking slowly along the edge of the road. I took water to her, but she'd been hurt by men before and she was afraid of me.

She pulled herself up a steep hill and went deeper into the woods.

Placing the water where she was standing moments before, I drove off a way and parked out of sight, to see if she came back. She didn't.

This exhausted dog, like so many out there, was journeying to that special place where someone would just be kind to her.

I returned over and over but never saw her there again.

About ten days later I was leaving the house and who do you think was coming up *my* dirt road?

Fifteen miles from where she first crossed the highway, Bebe was still searching for that special place that she knew in her heart was her reason for living ... that place where she would be wanted.

Bebe rested under a tree in my back yard!

She was here ... she drank some water that I left out for the rabbits, and while I was getting her a bowl of food, she left again.

I jumped into the four wheel drive and flew up the mountain. But Bebe was gone.

What had she suffered since I last saw her?

It was cold and the wind was gusting. I set up five feeding stations in the hills behind my house. They were made from old dog houses. Then I waited ... and hoped.

Over a week went by.

Finally, one morning, I found Bebe again, eating someone's trash. This spot was about two miles from my house. But Bebe spotted me and ran up into the hills and disappeared like a coyote! Next day I saw her again.

This time she ran into the mountains crossing someone's ranch. I approached the ranchers and asked if they knew Bebe.

They said she'd been eating their trash for a week, living in the mountains behind their home. If I set a trap for her, they would help me watch it.

So I set up the trap.

That first night, we caught her!

But she bent the metal door on our trap and escaped. She was determined to find that magical place in her heart and nothing would stop her.

I returned in an hour with a second trap.

Two days later we caught her again. And she tore the new trap apart and escaped again!

Bebe was struggling more than ever to get to this special place, and I found out why ...

... she was pregnant, and she wanted a better life for her children.

Days passed without seeing her at all. Had she been so frightened of us that she wouldn't come near us again?

Then one morning, after driving my daughter to her school, I saw a dog walking the center line on the highway.

Luckily, at that moment, no cars were coming.

I pulled over and got out and walked up to the dog. It was the now very pregnant Bebe.

She stood still on the road and looked at me ... a

knowing look ... then she walked slowly off into a field. I lost sight of her despite hours of searching.

Feeling weak and exhausted, I had become obsessed with saving this dog.

It was many weeks and I couldn't sleep at night ... neither could Bebe, who was now twenty miles from where I first saw her.

Worried about finding enough food for her developing kids, she kept searching for that special place. She knew it was finally close by. And she was exhausted and cold.

Later that same night, she walked into our trap again. She ate the food, and laid down to rest as the door closed. She didn't struggle, she just whimpered and hoped.

When I got to the trap and looked at her, poking a finger through the wire to touch her, she looked up and I could see the hope in her eyes ... the hope that this was that special place in her heart ... her destiny.

Days later Bebe had 11 healthy puppies, 6 boys and 5 girls.

I kept the whole family at home with me for the first four weeks. When I knew all were safe, I moved them to our Supershelter.

Bebe is one of our most special dogs. She's finally happy and loved ... at a very special place.

Chapter 16

*"Severely wounded, she
dragged herself to us for help."*

April, 1994

People like you helped save Little Debbie's life, because their gifts helped us create our unique "feeding stations" in the forest.

Little Debbie and her devoted brother were dumped in the forest, without anywhere to hide from its mortal dangers.

After days of hunger, and being near exhaustion, these two puppies found one of our feeding stations and made it their new home.

They lived under a bush next to the station.

But whenever I came near, Little Debbie ran off into the brush about fifty feet, and her brother stood between her and me ... barking ... to shield her.

Then, the worst happened ....

Early one morning, I found Little Debbie leaning up against our feeding station. She was bloody and weak.

She had been attacked by predators and was full of holes and gashes ... and she'd lost a lot of blood.

Bravely, she dragged herself to the only friendly

place she could think of ... our feeding station.

Frightened as she was, she was too weak to run away, so I was able to pick her up and carry her to our van.

I gave her emergency first aid and rushed her to our new shelter hospital.

I called ahead to alert our vet that we were on the way and that Little Debbie needed emergency care. Two park ranger friends of mine stayed behind to search for Little Debbie's brother.

By the evidence they found, it looks as though he tried to protect his sister ... barking and putting himself between her and the predators that attacked her.

But he was killed.

He died bravely defending the sister he loved so much ... our Little Debbie.

I prayed that she would live.

At our hospital, Little Debbie was put on an IV drip and got antibiotics as well as anti-shock drugs. She spent the next two days getting stabilized ... resting in her heated oxygen unit.

Days later, she had surgery for her wounds.

Soon she was feeling a lot better. But every time I went to touch her, she folded her head under her arm to protect herself ... as if I was going to hit her.

Her brother was gone, Little Debbie was in a strange new place ... and she was afraid.

But people were helping her, and they were being nice to her ... maybe for the first time in her short life.

After a few days, she let me touch her head. And one morning while I was stroking her face, telling her she was safe and loved, she reached over ... and kissed my fingers.

What a joy!

This morning, I took Little Debbie into one of our exercise yards and let her run and play.

She's much happier now. She smiles a lot and she loves to be hugged ... though she still has nightmares when she's asleep.

But she's going to make it!

Little Debbie is utter proof you can make the difference between life and death for these deserted animals.

We invented "feeding stations" ... and when she was near death, Little Debbie crawled to one of them ... for comfort.

Because we were there, this precious, loving puppy will live a long and happy life.

And every time I see her, I will thank her brave little brother who gave his life that she might live. And in my heart, I will hug him and tell him how his sacrifice did not go to waste.

I hope that, through Little Debbie, he will live with us and share her happiness.

Dear Leo,

My wife and I were on a tour of your Supershelter last month.

I had no idea how huge that place is!

When you say 750 dogs and cats, I figure, yeh, that's a lot. But when you see them, it's overwhelming.

How on earth do you take care of them all? They are all so happy and clean -- and well fed!

We expected the depressing "dog pound" look of other humane societies we've visited, but your place is so different from anything we ever imagined.

Now that I know where my donations go, I'm going to send you more every month.

I would be doing what you're doing in another life, thank God for you! The least I can do is send you regular monthly support.

My hat is off to you! Proof that one man can make a difference in this life.

Not one, but two hospitals! You amaze even me and I'm the head of a major corporation. If you ever want to do motivational seminars, I can get you booked across the country!

R.H.

Chapter 17

"She loved too much."

May, 1993

Mary Lou showed up at one of our forest feeding stations to eat her first real meal in weeks.

Her bones showed through her thin coat.

Without food or fat on her body, she spent many cold nights shivering, huddled in a ball.

She had dried, dark spray paint stuck to her sides.

Boxers are one breed of dog used as status symbols in certain neighborhoods. If a gang member has a boxer, he can parade her around wearing a spiked collar and demand "respect" from his peers.

If a dog doesn't live up to this fearsome image, if she embarrasses a gang member in front of his peers, he'd have to save face.

Knowing Mary Lou, I can guess what happened.

After being told how fierce this boxer was, some "macho" kid was determined to test her.

He mustered up his nerve and approached her, carefully. Taunting her, he called her by name. Without hesitating, Mary Lou exploded in seeming retaliation.

She jumped off her feet and lunged toward this now

frightened boy.

With both arms she reached for his face.

Pushing her weight off her hind legs she wrapped herself around his head and with her steaming hot muzzle against his neck she opened her mouth.

He could feel her teeth touching his bare throat.

He closed his eyes in fear and in anticipation of intense pain. Then, in an enormous burst of relief, he started laughing.

Mary Lou was licking his ear.

He laughed so hard he fell backwards onto the ground. Mary Lou followed him down, her arms clinging to his neck. She licked him, and licked him ... and wagged her tail while she licked him some more.

When she was finally pulled off this boy, he was still rolling on the ground, laughing. He hadn't had such a good time in years.

But he was "tough" ... he got up, and brushed himself off.

Maybe his friends jeered at him for being afraid. Or maybe for playing with a dog. Whatever happened, somebody was ridiculed into teaching Mary Lou a lesson.

Grabbing a can of spray paint, someone "tagged" her. Branded as "useless," Mary Lou was driven to the forest and dumped there ... left to die.

For weeks this heartsick dog roamed the brush searching for food and warmth.

When I rescued her, she seemed timid and exhausted. I carried her to our van. She looked up at me, blinked her eyes hopefully, then slept all the way to our shelter.

In the morning, I took Mary Lou for a walk in one of our huge exercise yards. I sat on a boulder watching her run around, a huge smile on her face.

Then she turned and jumped on me, knocking me off my rock!

Having me defenseless and on the ground, Mary Lou smothered me with kisses. She hugged and kissed me until I laughed so hard tears ran down my cheeks.

I sat up and hugged her back.

She kept slobbering me with kisses. Mary Lou discovered it was okay to love people again.

Looking into her eyes, I wondered: "What if I weren't there to rescue her?"

I could imagine Mary Lou walking until she dropped. Weak, trembling with cold, drifting off to sleep ... tears in her big brown eyes ... wondering why this was her fate.

Having done nothing wrong, only having loved too much ... her breaths would get shallower and shallower until she and her gift were carried off this undeserving planet.

Chills ran over me just thinking about it, watching this little girl smile.

But thanks to people like you, Mary Lou is alive. And she is safe and loved at our shelter.

Dear Leo,

You have inspired me to rescue animals from my local shelter.

I watched your "Safe House" video which shows us how to find homes for animals. I also got the booklet you sent with the tape telling me how I can save animals in my home town. That did the trick! Now that I know how to do it, I will!

Actually, I've often wondered about how I could help animals. Then, when I started donating to your group, I thought about starting one too. But it's so complicated, and such a responsibility -- how do you do it? You must never get a day off, let alone a vacation. How can you?

Anyway, even if I found others who wanted to help me, I like the idea of learning the ropes the way you suggest. Then if I fail, the animals won't suffer, I'll just keep the ones I rescued from the shelter.

Thanks for making that video. I have a new respect for those celebrities you have in the show too.

M.D.

Chapter 18

"The one who stole my heart."

October, 1992

In her seven short weeks of life, little "Peanut" went through some kind of hell.

I'll never know what really happened to this three pound puppy, but I can put the pieces together.

Peanut races around the floor in huge circles, then leaps up as high as she can with her little legs and bites onto whatever she finds ... my shirt, me ... whatever!

If you hold your hand out while she's in this puppy "playing" mode, she'll bite onto it and drag you around.

There isn't a mean bone in her body, she's just being a puppy. But being so tiny, her milk teeth are like needles. When she bites down, she can cut you.

I think she bit down on someone once too often and they reacted out of vengeance toward her.

However they did it, whatever they used, the pain was intense.

Before she could bark, Peanut's only sound was a

loud, blood-curdling scream.

Sitting in our living room the first time we heard it, my wife and I both ran to the kitchen, looking for an injured Peanut.

What we found was a cute little puppy with sad eyes wanting us to pick her up and hold her.

But the only sound she knew was this one. Not a whimper or a whine, or even a puppy bark ... but a loud shriek as if she were being tortured.

I keep imagining the violent pain she felt when it happened.

Then shivers run up and down my back and I can hear Peanut screaming out in anguish and terror in my mind ... when somebody got angry at her and cut off all the fingers on her left hand.

I want to stop it but I can't. Then it's over. I have a strange tightness in my stomach and I'm sweating.

There's a slight pressure on my foot, I look down, it's Peanut, she's smiling and tugging at my cuffs.

I pick her up and hold her tight. "Nobody will ever hurt you again little one," I think to myself. And she licks my nose.

Probably worried at having to explain what happened, the person who hurt Peanut decided to abandon her at a campsite in this wilderness area.

She was in a large box with her left paw crudely wrapped when I first saw her.

Peanut had been out all night in the cold, huddled in the far corner of her box. Through some miracle, she'd survived both exposure and the hungry displaced coyotes, who apparently didn't see her.

I picked Peanut up and tucked her in under my chin. She's been there ever since.

This little girl's courage moved me so much I promised her the best life I could dream up ... and I'd work everyday at trying to give it to her.

So I'm keeping her myself.

Thank you for helping me be there for Peanut ... but most of all ... thank you for Peanut.

Peanut epilog,

For over two years Peanut has been our most spoiled kid ever.

She sleeps between Stacy and myself, and sometimes on my pillow. Of course, I spend all night holding her and letting her drink from a special glass of water I bring to bed just for her.

If I go to bed and forget the water, she stands on my chest and whines while looking at where the water should be on the night stand next to the bed.

When this happens, I have to get up, get a fresh glass of water and bring it back to bed. Peanut has a few sips and then settles in for the night.

When I'm on the phone, she's in my lap. At fifteen pounds, she's just heavy enough to make my legs go to sleep. So part of the time, I'm holding her in my arms instead.

And she gets kissed at least five hundred times a day!

Peanut is spoiled ... and it's my sincere pleasure in being able to do it. And when I think of what happened, I thank God for this mission and for leading me to her.

She is an absolute joy. And to think someone had this diamond, and threw her away!

Chapter 19

"Cold, hungry and wet."

January, 1993

It was bone-chilling cold and raining heavily at the ocean camp site.

Scampering among the bushes, stopping only to sniff bits of trash she might eat, was tiny Little Edith ... the smallest four month old kitten I've ever seen.

Stunted from lack of food, this bony little girl caught the scent of fresh "Sheba" cat food coming from one of my rescue traps.

She ate her way into the cage, but her tiny stomach filled up quickly on the bite-sized morsels and she backed out again before I could catch her.

Searching for Edith in the bushes, I saw a flash of white socks among the green leaves. These feet were too big to be Edith's ... it had to be a litter mate's.

I ran around to the other side of the bush and waited for her to appear ....

All summer long vacationers from all over the country abandon their unwanted cats at this primitive campground. When the campers stop coming each fall, those poor, frightened animals that are left behind, slowly starve ... or die of exposure and disease.

But thanks to the support of people like yourself, I can save the cats left at this site each season.

After about ten minutes, the other kitten I named Beatrice, came out of the bush ... her hunger overcame her fear for the moment. She was gray and white, and her little body shivered in the cold rain.

She paused a moment and looked over her shoulder and blinked at me ... as if to thank me for caring enough to help her.

Then she went back into the bush to rest and lick the water off her muddy coat. Beatrice was too weak to walk the ten feet to my trap, so I pushed it into the bush.

The rain got worse. Tired and soaked, Beatrice would catch pneumonia if I couldn't help her.

For about an hour I wiped the rain from my face as I circled the giant thirty foot wide bush hoping for her to come out.

Then, I came around a bend and my heart pounded with excitement. Beatrice was in my trap, the door closed and she was eating furiously.

Even when I ran up to the cage, she couldn't stop eating. I watched her little belly balloon out from her ribs ... she was twice the size of her tiny sister, but Beatrice was just as thin.

Quickly, I put a towel over the cage.

She cowered in fear as I moved her into the van to keep her warm. There was still no sign of the tiny one I named Little Edith.

Minutes later I unexpectedly caught another kitten, a little boy.

Darkness was threatening when I finally saw Little Edith again.

I think she knew she might be left behind. She came out of the bush and dashed under a picnic table, heading right for my trap.

This time she ate *all* the food and the cage door closed behind her. She was safe ... she could come home with us!

Little Edith was probably as relieved as I was.

What a gift!

After all the cold rain and my sneezing, I had my prizes ... three frightened, sick kittens who wouldn't have lasted a few more days.

I was overcome with feelings of relief and joy.

I'm so lucky to be a part of their lives ... even a small part. To be able to make a difference for them. To be their friend.

Frightened, my three kittens huddled in the backs of their cages on the drive to our shelter.

I was able to rescue Edith, Beatrice, their brother and eventually the other seven members of their family.

They are all recovering together at our Supershelter hospital.

This work can continue only as long as people like you are a part of it. Please consider joining our mission. Send a gift to help save abandoned animals, today.

Dear Leo,

I just recently began donating to D.E.L.T.A. Rescue and I must tell you, I am surprised!

Every month when your update comes, I can't wait to read a wonderful story of an animal my previous donation helped to rescue.

I really feel like I'm part of this mission. Your letters make me feel like I'm out there with you, by your side.

Unlike so many others who ask me to "join" their group and then just send me a magazine or a newsletter, you really have animals! I know where my gifts go when I send them to you.

I'm in love with your organization! Can you tell?! My husband is too, and he doesn't like any of them!

Do you know how hard it is to get personal attention these days? When I send a gift to you, you thank me within days and I feel really good about myself for helping.

I think everyone who wants to feel good about themselves should donate to D.E.L.T.A. Rescue.

You can publish this note in your "Dear Leo" column if you like -- I want everyone to know how special you are. Your cheerleader,

T.D.H.

Chapter 20

*"She thought I was going
to hit her like the others."*

November, 1994

Imagine a beautiful and loving young girl ... taken for a ride and thrown out of a car at a wilderness campsite ... left to go hungry, shiver in the cold, and die.

Well, you don't have to imagine it ... this horror happened to our new red puppy, "Cicely."

But she didn't die.

Thanks to people like you, I rescued Cicely in her hour of desperation, and took her to our beautiful 89-acre mountain-top sanctuary, where we both fell in love.

At first, Cicely didn't trust anyone ... not even me.

Then something happened ....

Arriving at our hospital after a long drive, I put Cicely down for a minute while I prepared her vaccination. She immediately wet the floor.

But as soon as she finished, she curled up into a ball and her little body trembled with fright.

Seeing this, I reached down to pet her and tell her it was okay. When I did, she winced ... raising her paw to protect her face.

She thought she was going to be hit.

I swallowed hard to keep the tears down, and I picked Cicely up and hugged her tight.

"It's okay honey," I told her, "nobody's going to hurt you ever again."

Cicely understood me ... she looked at me with those warm, brown eyes and then she kissed my face.

Since that day, whenever she sees me Cicely rolls over on her back, wags her tail and waits for me to rub her tummy. Then she runs in circles around me, stops suddenly and stands up on my leg so I can pat her head.

She gets so excited when she sees me, it's contagious! I get excited to see her too, and I have to stop whatever I'm doing to play with her.

What does that mean ... when two people get all excited to see each other and share the joy in being together?

Well, animals are people too! They speak a different language and have a different culture, but they are people just like us.

They think and feel and love ... just like us.

So Cicely and I fell in love. She's happiest when I cradle her in my arms and hug her. And I'm sure if you saw her, you'd feel the same about her.

Without us, this loving little puppy would not have lasted even a few days. Hunger, exposure and predators would have claimed Cicely. It was a close call for her.

I shudder to think what her frightening and painful final moments would have been like, without our help.

Chapter 21

"They said he was ugly and they wouldn't touch him."

April, 1993

"Bobby" was cowering when I first met him.

His body was covered with tiny white flakes and his hair was thin all over.

A bald patch of erupted skin ringed his neck about six inches wide ... he looked so bad everyone who saw him was afraid to go near him.

Bobby was quiet, and resigned to being treated as a "leper" ... nobody wanting to touch him.

There are two kinds of dog mange. One is easily cured but is highly contagious. Not contagious, but harder to rid, is the other kind of mange. Without a microscope you can't tell which is which.

Whichever one it was, I didn't want Bobby to feel he was being quarantined, so I let him walk around loose inside our rescue van. I would disinfect it later.

Then I drove off to our shelter.

It takes about an hour to get there from this section of the forest, and Bobby leaned up against the seat and looked out the window. He was sad and depressed.

I made up a bunch of names and called him by them, but there was no response.

Then I said "Bobby" and he came over to me slowly. He put his head down and stopped about three feet from me while I was driving.

His loneliness was too much to bear. My heart melted for him.

Then I realized what was going on. This poor cocker-mix young boy had not been touched or petted in months.

Everyone was afraid of catching something from him. So he was discarded in the forest, "out of sight, out of mind."

Realizing his emotional pain, I called Bobby closer. I wanted to hug him tight and comfort him, but I was driving. But I managed to rub his head and neck, and massage his itchy skin.

Bobby closed his eyes and turned his head into my hand. It felt good. Somebody loved him again.

After a few minutes, Bobby wagged his tail at me and let me pet his whole body, all the while keeping his eyes closed as if he was in some far off place.

Was he dreaming of his mother, the last one to really love him, wishing it was her again?

Or was he just enjoying it, basking in the love that was pouring out onto him?

Driving with my left hand, petting Bobby with my right, we eventually got to our shelter and our new hospital. Bobby got a physical and his shots, and it turned out he didn't even have mange. Instead he had a skin condition caused by a vitamin deficiency.

He was probably eating garbage for so long his body began falling apart.

Bobby instantly became the darling of our shelter. Everyone wanted to love him and play with him when they heard that nobody went near him ... for months.

Imagine what Bobby thought. Every time he looked at someone, they threatened to harm him if he came near.

What a tortured life, what a feeling of worthlessness.

But thanks to you, I was able to be there to rescue Bobby and now we're showering him with hugs and attention.

He smiles and jumps with joy, and his hair is growing back too!

Bobby is living proof of the difference our love can make ... and the difference you can make to an abandoned animal with no hope of survival, wondering why his perfect love has been rejected.

Bobby is always smiling now, jumping up for everyone to pet him. He's forgotten his troubles and he's happy again. People like you made the difference. Please continue the miracles.

Dear Reader,

For all the animals I told you about, there are hundreds of others that are alive today because of people like you.

Many who were rescued were adopted by D.E.L.T.A. Rescue supporters and lived happily ever after with their loving new families.

I hope you can tell how much I love these animals ... my life is dedicated to their rescue and care.

But without people like you, none of these stories would have a happy ending. All of these wonderful animals would have suffered and died ... alone ... in the wilderness.

Thank God for the many folks who have joined me in helping these abandoned cats and dogs.

Won't you please become one of them?

When you do, I will write to you each month to tell you about another animal's rescue. And you can tour our 89-acre no-kill Supershelter to see our precious animals in person.

Please ... help me continue my war on abandonment ... send a tax-deductible gift today.

For the animals,
Leo Grillo

EPILOG

I can't believe, at the dawn of a new millennium when we expected to be riding in Jetson-style space vehicles and cars with air jets instead of wheels ... nothing has changed, really.

We are still so backward as to condone, by our apathy, animal cruelty.

I don't get it. With all the huge national humane organizations, we still have brutal puppy mills; animal sacrifices in the name of "freedom of religion;" barbaric vivisection in the name of medicine and cosmetics; and people are giving up their pet-children in record-breaking numbers.

I have a shadow, a side-kick, a partner, a pal, a "son" who is always at my feet or sitting next to me: my terrier-poodle, Fred.

Fred is totally committed to being with me, even when my odd hours keep him awake through the night.

His love is unconditional and his friendship is priceless.

How can people who have their own Freds, suddenly decide to "get rid of him?"

How is that possible?

Ghandi is quoted often, by animal rights advocates, as saying that you can judge a society by the way it treats its animals.

I'd like to propose the axiom that *we can't*

save this society, on its present course, until we begin saving the animals.

To put it another way, if we develop the compassion to care about innocent animals ... dogs, cats, horses, farm animals, wild animals, a mouse, a snake, a bunny, a robin ... and we help them to survive on this harsh planet, then maybe someday we will learn to develop that same compassion for our fellow humans.

Until that day comes, people like you and me have to team up and become an army to fight for these animals ... to help them have a fruitful life of their own, free from suffering, especially that imposed by man.

By our words and especially by our actions, we must teach the rest of the world what we know about these magnificent beings with whom we share this planet.

I'm asking you to join with me by sending a gift to help rescue animals abandoned in the wilderness. This is the *emergency* we must respond to first. These animals need food and water ... *today*. They need a place to sleep, protection form injury and disease ... *today*.

If we can solve this one problem, we will inspire others to save animals too.

They have discovered that criminals were cruel to animals as children. What if all children were kind to animals? What would society become in twenty years?

We must teach them, *by our actions*. Please use the coupons at the back of this book to wage war against animal suffering. Please join this mission, today.

The History of D.E.L.T.A. Rescue

1979

Leo Grillo, a Hollywood actor, found 35 dogs starving in the wilderness outside of Los Angeles. Without food or shelter, their lives depended on Grillo's daily feeding. Grillo learned to medicate these dogs in the field when they were sick.

1980

Grillo leased kennel space and rescued those 35 dogs and about three dozen more who were abandoned during that first year. He found homes for most of them, but kept about twenty because they were abused and unwanted. Grillo realized that most shelters would kill those remaining dogs, but he refused saying that "these animals are people too!"

1982

Dedication & Everlasting Love To Animals is incorporated as a non-profit organization in California and becomes a federally tax-exempt no-kill organization the same year. Grillo chose the name to match the acronym "D.E.L.T.A.," which was the name of his own beloved dog.

1983

Besides the scores he had in leased kennels, Grillo fed over 150 dogs in the forest, and 29 dogs and 12 cats at his house. Clearly he needed his own shelter. So he set out to find one. In October he purchased a 50 year-old kennel in El Monte, California, which he cleaned up himself. It was this humble shelter that became home to 250 rescued dogs and cats.

1985

By now, *Dedication & Everlasting Love To Animals* had acquired a national reputation by bringing to the forefront the plight of abandoned animals. Grillo also acquired a ranch near Acton, California, to house 60 rescued feral cats as well as rescued livestock, horses and burros.

1986

The first 23-acres of the "Supershelter" were acquired. Immediately, its 2500 square foot home was converted into a 5,000 square foot indoor cattery. He built the first of many spacious dog yards with insulated clubhouses and wading pools for his rescues.

1988

With permission from the State of California, Grillo rescued over 80 cats from a popular seaside resort and ended a 25-year abandonment problem there.

1990

Grillo formed the educational division "D.E.L.T.A. Productions" and produced the video SAFE HOUSE. Later, Grillo founded a new educational non-profit and produced the D.E.L.T.A. Rescue Story TV show.

1991

A new state of the art, 2500 square foot veterinary hospital was built at the Supershelter. It was only for D.E.L.T.A. Rescue's animals, but was soon filled. Grillo also founded Horse Rescue of America as a non-profit organization to rescue horses and burros.

1993

"Dog Town," a prototype of the "shelter of the future" was created, complete with heated and cooled in-ground dog houses and large yards for each pair of dogs to enjoy. Also a second 2500 square foot hospital building was constructed to relieve overcrowding in the first. All animals are treated at D.E.L.T.A. Rescue, even cancer or other chronic patients.

Today!

D.E.L.T.A. Rescue has over 140 acres of land, and houses over 500 dogs and 250 cats in three no-kill shelters. The Supershelter is now 89 acres of sanctuary. Livestock and other animals have a place to live out their lives as well. To educate the public about the plight of abandoned animals, a new TV show is in development. Twelve new catteries were just opened and plans are under way to build more Dog Towns! At 46 years old, Grillo provides leadership for D.E.L.T.A. Rescue, does all the rescuing and fund raising himself, and plans on continuing as President, as he has for over 15 years.

D.E.L.T.A. Rescue depends entirely on donations from individuals like yourself. We rescue dogs and cats who are abandoned in the wilderness, left to starve to death.

We have over 750 loving animals at a time at our 89-acre no-kill sanctuary. Won't you please join this mission of mercy today?

Yes, Leo! I want to help save animals like those in this book, abandoned in the wilderness. Here's my gift to spend over the next month ...

❏ $20 ❏ $30 ❏ $50 ❏ $90 $250 ❏ $_____

Your Name: _____

Your Address: _____

City & State: _____

Zip: _____

Please make your check payable to: **D.E.L.T.A. Rescue** *or use your credit card. Mail to the address on the back of this page.*

❏ Visa ❏ Master Card ❏ American Express ❏ Discover

☐☐☐☐ ☐☐☐☐ ☐☐☐☐ ☐☐☐☐

Signature: _____ Expires: _____

Please mail this coupon to:

**D.E.L.T.A. Rescue
PO Box 9
Glendale, CA 91209**

Preface to Guide

Do you know that the average stay of a pet in a home today is only two and a half years? That's why over twenty million animals a year show up in pounds and humane societies ... and in the wilderness.

For many years, people have been calling me to ask if I would take their pet ... whom they no longer want.

In the beginning, I became a screaming madman over the phone ... this was like someone calling to give up their child! How could they?

To save my voice, I wrote this *Pet Adoption Guide* and sent it for free to anyone who asked.

Later, I made a video tape called "Safe House" which is this guide brought to TV. Some celebrity friends agreed to join me and appeared in Safe House. It is very entertaining, as well as educational.

If you would like a copy of the video, Safe House, please send in the coupon at the back of this book. Meanwhile, use the following written guide to place the pets you rescue.

This guide is also available as a booklet. If you want to help animals in your home town, order some booklets and give them to people who are advertising "Free Pets" in your local newspaper.

If you show them how to find *safe* new homes for their pets, two things will happen. *First*, they will screen potential new homes better. And *second*, they may feel that the whole process is too complicated ... and decide to keep their animal!

Pet Adoption Guide

How to find a loving new home for a beloved pet or rescued animal

Use this section when you want to find a pet a good home ....

You'll find a lot of information in these pages... please take the time to look it over... and digest it.

But also understand that it's impossible to acquire years of experience by reading one booklet. The information we offer is a *set of guidelines* - intended only to lead you down the right path.

If you've just rescued a poor little dog or cat... then congratulations!! You are one of the few willing to put yourself out and give him a second chance.

The "humane societies" are filled and will most likely put your rescue "to sleep" (kill him) if you take him there. You must know this already or you wouldn't be doing this adoption yourself.

If you don't have much time or a place to keep your charge, board him in a kennel for a couple of weeks until you find him that new home. You can find kennels listed under "Dog Boarding" or "Dog Kennels" in the yellow pages. Visit the kennel first and be sure it is well run; inspect all the dog and cat areas to be sure they look OK. And don't forget to visit this animal!

Why you must do this yourself ....

Unfortunately, you can't just call some "animal group" and think it will take over your problem.

Legitimate organizations have many animals and

don't have the money - or the time, either - to take an extra one.

Nationally, only five percent of all pets given to a shelter are adopted to a new home. The other 95% are eventually killed. *That's 19 out of 20!*

How do they die?

Your pet could end up in a laboratory - especially if he's a "nice" pet (one that won't bite when stuck with a needle or cut without anesthetic.)

He could end up on someone's table - as dinner.

He could be beaten into "guard" duty.

He could be abused sexually by sick human beings before being tortured to death.

MOST LIKELY this lovable pet will be killed by the humane society itself because nobody will adopt him in time.

These atrocities are being committed every day, and your pet could be the next victim - there's a 95% chance he will be!!

Lost or Abandoned?

You must first decide if your rescue is just "lost" or actually abandoned.

If he looks healthy, happy and fat, place "FOUND" ads in your local newspaper and put up signs on trees and sign posts in the area where you found him. But if he is in poor shape - thin, worn, etc. - he has probably been abandoned. Look through back issues of your local newspapers for "LOST" ads that might fit his description, anyway.

When you are sure the animal is not just lost and that an owner cannot be found, proceed with the "Steps to Finding a Loving New Home" on the next page.

What about the "pound?"

Even when the local pound says it's the law that you must bring animals in... many people don't!!

First of all, it's usually *not* the law!

It's just the pound's way of intimidating people into bringing in these animals. Why? MONEY!!

Pounds get paid for each animal they house by the city they operate under; they get money by the ton from rendering companies that want animal carcasses for use in products; and they get money from you when you bail the pet out again after the required waiting period. If you do all you can to get the pet back to his owner - signs, ads, etc. - the pound can't do much more.

Steps To Finding A Loving New Home

1. If you haven't done so already, get to a vet! You must have shots and a clean bill of health for your animal. This is a *must* today. A new family doesn't want to fall in love with a pet only to suffer the heartbreak of his dying of some common preventable disease.

2. Place a paid classified ad in your area newspaper. "Your area" is defined as your immediate geographic surroundings, with a total population of at least 100,000. There is usually at least one major newspaper in each area of that size. Your area may be a few square miles in a major city or many square miles in the country.

3. When you place your classified ad, BE CREATIVE. Speak in HUMAN TERMS. Describe your pet by personality traits and habits. The breed or closest breed that describes your pet's appearance should head the ad. The following is an example of an ad, but you can probably think of an even better one:

ADORABLE GERMAN SHEPHERD MIX.
Loves soft music, strawberry ice cream and gentle petting. Three years old, spayed and very loyal. Please open your heart to her. Call 555-5555.

4. Do not advertise a price on your pet. Let them guess if there is one and how much... the first step is to get the calls.

5. *SUCCESS!!* People are calling your ad... many, many people! *Be careful now!* Take the names and numbers of all the callers and tell them you'll get back to them in an hour. DO NOT answer any questions!

Why are we doing it this way? Many people, up to no good, will not leave a number or will leave a wrong number. You can only imagine whom you have avoided in this way... a lab dealer collecting animals to sell, meat buyers, back yard breeders or puppy mills, etc.

If you are shy and can't tell people to wait for your call, tell them a white lie! "The dog belongs to my brother and he's not here right now. If you'll leave your name and number he'll call you back in an hour or so... "No, I'm just visiting and I don't know anything about his dog."

6. The trick to returning the phone calls is to ASK QUESTIONS IMMEDIATELY. They will try to ask you what kind of dog it is, etc. DON'T LET THIS HAPPEN. *You* ask the questions! Keep asking the questions and *keep the flow going*. The questions to ask are listed on the following pages. How to ask them is where your cleverness comes in.

EXAMPLE:

"I'm returning your call about the German shepherd; do you have a dog now? ... How long have you had her? ... Two years - that's wonderful! Did you have a dog before her? ... How long? ..." etc., etc.

7. Placement questions will draw out people's intentions for your beloved animal. Place him ONLY after you are sure the people have a loving home and will treat your cat or dog as a family member.

It's amazing how you can get people to voluntarily tell you what they intend. The questions on the following pages will help you develop a scenario for your phone conversations. Do most of your interviewing BY PHONE. It saves the pressure and embarrassment of eye-to-eye contact, especially when you say NO!!

Telephone Interview Scorecard

The responses to the following placement questions are rated with numbers. Plus signs correspond to positive feelings, minus to negative feelings, and the higher the number the stronger the feeling.

These numbers are based on my personal feelings; yours may vary in value. But think about *why* I placed each value - you'll find it's all a "gut" feeling, and the numbers only help define those feelings. Add up all points and compare to the ratings on page 113.

1. *Do you have a dog or cat now?*

   Yes..................... +1   No......................... 0

2. *If yes, how long have you had him?*

   0-3 yrs....... 0   3-6 yrs....... +2   6+ yrs...... +3

   If no, when is the last time you had one?

   How long did you have him?

   0-3 yrs....... 0   3-6 yrs....... +2   6+ yrs....... +3

3. *If you have a dog now, what size is he?*
   Yours is large, theirs is small........................ -10

(Will yours be the guard dog?)
Yours is large, theirs is large..............+2

Yours is small, theirs is large.............. -10
(Possible injury to your animal.)

Yours is small, theirs is small.............. +2

4. *If the animal is gone, what happened to him?*

Gave to friends.... -5   Gave to pound..... -10

Died of disease (under 3 yrs.)...................... -3

Did he have shots?............................... No: -10

Died of disease (3-9 yrs.).............................. -2

Died of disease (10+ yrs.)............................. 0
Died of congenital problem........................... 0

Ran away.................. PASS ON THEM NOW!!

Killed in traffic.......... PASS ON THEM NOW!!

Poisoned.................... If they live in the same house, PASS NOW!

5. *Do you have a fenced-in yard?*

Yes...................... +1   No...................... -10

6. *If yes, how high?*

2-4'....... -2   4-5'..... 0   6' & over....... +3

Does it drop to 4' at the gate and not separate from the back yard?

Yes...................... -2   No......................... 0

(Even if they claim to have a fence 6' high all around, it may drop to 4' or less at the gate - by city ordinance. In this case be sure the back yard is *separate* from the front yard, has a 6 ft gate and that it is a true 6' minimum.)

7. *Are there holes in the fence:*

Yes.................... -5   No...................... +1
(They must be repaired before you place your animal here.)

8. *Can a dog or cat dig under?*

Yes..................... -5   No...................... +1

9. *What kind of fence is it?*

Block wall.... +4   Chain link... +5   Wood.... -5

(note: in earthquake country, block walls come tumbling down, only chain link remains in most cases.)

10. *Where will the pet sleep?*

Indoors....... +3   Outdoors...... -3   Both...... 0

11. *Will this be an indoor or outdoor pet?*

DOG: Indoor..... +3   Outdoor..... -3   Both.... 0

CAT: Indoor only... +5   Outdoor or In/Out... -10

12. *Who is your veterinarian?*

Gives a veterinarian's name .... +2

Has none or can't remember the name .... -2

13. *Will you spay or neuter the pet within 30 days?*

Yes.............. +4   No (or hesitant) .... -10
(If this is a full grown animal, you should do this before you adopt him.)

14. *Is/was your other pet spayed/neutered?*

Yes...................... +4   No...................... -10

15. *Have you had your cat(s) tested for FeLv (feline leukemia) and FIV?*

Yes...................... +3   No...................... -10

(Never place an FIV or FeLv positive cat with a negative cat, it's a DEATH SENTENCE for both! Get a test on your cat and, if negative, let the prospective owners show you a negative test on their cat(s) performed within the last 30 days. If your cat is positive, try to keep him because he's going to die soon and the stress of leaving you will kill him quicker.)

Next we are going to add up the points and make sense of the feelings. See if your interpretation agrees with mine. Along the way you have begun to know your people - they have revealed themselves and their intentions to you. You have probably already decided whether or not you want to continue with them. When you find someone you want to go ahead with, continue with the big step, Step 8 (next page).

RATING

Add and subtract the points. Remember that these numbers represent feelings. You either have a good prospect or a terrible one. For me, four out of five calls are *NOT WORTH PROCEEDING WITH*. So don't be discouraged - and above all don't panic and give the animal away just because you think you won't get another call! You'll always get more calls!!

TOTAL POINTS   INTERPRETATION

30-37   Probably a very good home. Invite them over to see your pet.

21-30   Hold out for more calls.

Below 21   DON'T EVEN THINK ABOUT IT!!

END OF TELEPHONE INTERVIEW SECTION

Please continue on to step 8

8. You've just talked to some nice people and you want to invite them over. First you must whet their appetites. Don't tell them too much about your pet... they just talked themselves hoarse so time is on your side! Tell them a few highlights and get

right to the invitation.

I usually tell them I have the perfect animal for them (and I usually do!), so "Can you come over the day after tomorrow at such and such a time?" I try to make it a little inconvenient and at least 48 hours later. That way they are truly "planning" on finding a new pet. What's a few hours when they're embarking on a full 15-year commitment?

9. So you've set the appointment; the couple (there should generally be a family-type of situation here) comes to meet their prospective new family member. You invite them into your yard or your living room and engage in some small talk, going over key points again. So far, they haven't seen your pet.

Go over the fact that you want to "deliver" your pet to them if it works out. Tell them you want him back if it doesn't work out - even in five years! (You don't want this poor animal to go through this same thing all over again.)

Tell them you *don't* want the pet given away to anyone else... he must come back to you first for your "approval" of the possible transfer. If they have any present intention of giving the pet away after they get him from you, catch them now and THROW THEM OUT!! People are VERY SWEET when they want something, but you will be up against some VERY NASTY characters later if something is wrong.

10. After you are sure these are your people, tell them about your pet and see if they act warmly and smile as you talk. They should be anticipating your pet's arrival - if so they will be excited and warm looking. If not, be careful; this is a big moment... why aren't they excited? What's going on?

11. Now you finally bring your pet out to meet his potential new family. WATCH THEIR EYES - CLOSELY. *This is perhaps the single most important SECRET OF ADOPTING pets to good homes.* The moment they see your pet, you should be looking at their eyes. It happens in a flash... one second or less!

All eyes should be smiling. If *anyone* has a puzzled look, a disappointed look, or a clinical, uncaring look, *you should be planning your escape strategy.* If, for example, the husband loves the pet but the wife appears hesitant, PASS ON BOTH.

"Escape strategy" is what you use to get them out of your house *without* your dog or cat. Usually you can say that someone else is coming over tomorrow and that you'll let the "winner" know in a day or so.

11. Let us assume we have a winner - a match between your pet and a LOVING new family. After about 20 minutes you should go over what your pet eats, what special habits he has, what treats he likes, etc. You should also explain that you want a spay/neuter certificate from their vet within 30 days (you should have one already if this pet is not a puppy or kitten).

13. You probably have a collar and tag on your pet. If not, buy one before you deliver him. Also, buy a tag for the new owners as a present to them. But, put your number on it next to theirs in case the pet gets out - that way you'll get a call too. (*You'd be surprised how many people lose their pet and don't want to tell you... meanwhile you've had him back for weeks!*)

14. Tell these people that you would like a donation of at least $50 to cover some of the vet bills you've run up for your pet's shots and the like. If they refuse, go into your exit strategy. The money is to ensure that they can afford to care for your pet. It's also to prevent "bunchers" from selling your pet to laboratory research dealers. Bunchers currently get about $65 or more for a "nice" pet for research.

15. If everyone, especially your pet, is happy, then arrange to deliver the animal. Aim to deliver him on a Saturday morning so he can spend the entire weekend with his new family. And don't deliver him at night because there is a reason you are there!

You are delivering your pet in daylight because these people may have lied or exaggerated some things about their residence. Ask for a tour of the animal's "sleeping quarters," etc. They have had time to buy his dishes and food, so you should see these also. If something is wrong, if they've made no preparations, ask why not. If you're suspicious, take your pet and run NOW before it's too late!

16. If all is well and you *and your pet* are happy with the new family, ask to have "visitation rights." Anyone on the level insists that you visit... they are now your friends.

17. You should feel good that you saved a life and found a new family for this pet. You'll also feel sad because you'll miss him. You'll keep re-living those precious moments of his rescue, his care... then his adoption. If you do this a thousand times, you'll still feel sad when you adopt one out. But you did it the right way to ensure his safety. Go home and have a good cry, you deserve it. But then do it again next week. The pounds are full of pets literally dying to get adopted.

Beware!!

Con men call ads in the paper pretending to be from "humane organizations." They will offer to find your pet a good home... to save you the bother of doing it yourself.

These people know human nature... we avoid hard work. We'd pay a "donation" to anyone willing to help us with our problems.

These con men make money by pretending to be "do-gooders," when in fact they brutally KILL YOUR PET the day they receive him. They can collect donations and pets all day long!!

Real humane groups are overcrowded and NEVER solicit for pets unless they too are fronts for money-making operations. There are some very large operations of this type advertising for donations to carry on this "wonderful" work. BEWARE.

And don't do "third party" adoptions. When someone says "It's for my dear sweet invalid mother..." or "It's for a friend..." use your exit strategy.

Also remember, young single people are not good prospects for a long-term relationship with your pet. Their lives change too rapidly, and what happens when they "meet someone" who doesn't like pets?

About the Author

Leo Grillo found three dozen dogs in the Angeles National Forest one autumn day in 1979. He phoned every humane organization in Los Angeles for help - but got none.

The "legitimate" groups were full and the others eventually would have killed his dogs.

Grillo decided to feed his new friends daily, in the forest, medicate them when they got sick, and find them new homes. It took a year, but he was successful.

Later, in 1982, he founded his non-profit *Dedication & Everlasting Love To Animals* (D.E.L.T.A. Rescue) to continue saving thousands of abandoned dogs and cats in the forest.

Today, D.E.L.T.A. RESCUE has three "no-kill" animal shelters housing more than 750 rescued animals, and relies totally on donations from people like you to keep these animals alive.

Grillo has appeared on national television numerous times, including multiple appearances on the Today Show, David Horowitz's Fight Back, Purina's Special Friends, Disney's Epcott Magazine, Newscope, CNN, National Geographic, etc.

To get extra copies of this book, write to: **D.E.L.T.A. Rescue, PO Box 9, Dept. XB, Glendale, CA 91209.**

To fight this war against the suffering of animals abandoned in the wilderness, we need to amass a giant army.

Please help us recruit new soldiers by sending us the name and address of someone who you know would like to have a **FREE COPY** of this book.

Just fill out the coupon below and *mail it to us at the address on the back side of this page.*

Please send a copy of this book to:

Name: _____

Address: _____

City & State: _____

Zip: _____

This Free Book was sent to you from:

Your Name: _____

Your Address: _____

City & State: _____

Zip: _____

Please mail this coupon to:

**D.E.L.T.A. Rescue
Free Book
PO Box 9
Glendale, CA 91209**

If you want to donate a number of books to your organization, club, association or to your local school library for the children to read, please fill out the coupon below.

Any size donation to help defray the cost of sending these books would be appreciated.

Please send _____ copies of *"Is This The Place?"* to:

Name of group: _____

Address: _____

City & State: _____

Zip: _____

These books were sent to you from:

Your Name: _____

Your Address: _____

City & State: _____

Zip: _____

(Please send this coupon along with any size gift to the address on the back of this page.)

Please mail this coupon to:

**D.E.L.T.A. Rescue
Book Donation
PO Box 9
Glendale, CA 91209**

If you would like a copy of our video "SAFE HOUSE: How to find a loving new home for your pet or rescued animal" please fill in the coupon below and *mail it to the address on the back of this page.*

Included with SAFE HOUSE is a free guide to help you rescue pets in your home town.

Celebrities in this show include: Dee Wallace Stone, Loretta Swit, Cleveland Amory, Bernie Kopell, David Horowitz, George Putnam, Earl Holliman and others.

Please send _____ copies of the video tape "SAFE HOUSE" to me at the address below:

Your Name: _____

Your Address: _____

City & State: _____

Zip: _____

I have included a donation of $_____ to help offset costs.

Please mail this coupon to:

**D.E.L.T.A. Rescue
SAFE HOUSE
PO Box 9
Glendale, CA 91209**

D.E.L.T.A. Rescue depends entirely on donations from individuals like yourself. We rescue dogs and cats who are abandoned in the wilderness, left to starve to death.

We have over 750 loving animals at a time at our 89-acre no-kill sanctuary. Won't you please join this mission of mercy today?

Yes, Leo! I want to help save animals like those in this book, abandoned in the wilderness. Here's my gift to spend over the next month ...

❏ $20 ❏ $30 ❏ $50 ❏ $90 $250 ❏ $_____

Your Name: _____

Your Address: _____

City & State: _____

Zip: _____

Please make your check payable to: **D.E.L.T.A. Rescue** *or use your credit card. Mail to the address on the back of this page.*

❏ Visa ❏ Master Card ❏ American Express ❏ Discover

Signature: _____ Expires: _____

_____

Please mail this coupon to:

**D.E.L.T.A. Rescue
Dept. CB
PO Box 9
Glendale, CA 91209**